Where's Your Dad?

Where's your dad?

My dad's at home.

My dad's working
at home.

Where's your mom?

My mom's at the market.

My mom's shopping
at the market.

Where's your brother?

My brother's at school.

My brother's studying at school.

Where's your sister?

My sister's
at the bookstore.

My sister's reading
at the bookstore.

Where's your uncle?

My uncle's
at the beach.

My uncle's napping
at the beach.

Where's your aunt?

My aunt's at the gym.

My aunt's running
at the gym.

Where are you?

I'm at the playground.

I'm playing
at the playground.

Let's learn more about Christmas.

Color the Christmas tree.